The Library of the Five Senses & the Sixth Sense™

Hearing

Sue Hurwitz

The Rosen Publishing Group's
PowerKids Press™
New York

Published in 1997 by The Rosen Publishing Group, Inc.
29 East 21st Street, New York, NY 10010

First Edition

Book Design: Kim Sonsky

Photo Credits: Cover and all photo illustrations by Seth Dinnerman.

Hurwitz, Sue, 1934–
    Hearing / by Sue Hurwitz.
        p.   cm. — (Library of the five senses [plus the sixth sense]
    Includes index.
    Summary: Explains the sense of hearing, including how the ear works.
    ISBN 0-8239-5056-5
    1. Hearing—Juvenile literature. [1. Hearing. 2. Ear. 3. Senses and sensation.] I. Title. II. Series: Hurwitz, Sue,
    1934– Library of the five senses (& the sixth sense)
    QP462.2.H87 1997
    612.8'5—dc21
                                         96–54499
                                            CIP
                                            AC

Manufactured in the United States of America

CONTENTS

Jeff

Jeff listened to the sounds from outside his bedroom. He heard birds singing in the tree by his window. He heard dogs barking in his yard. He heard the telephone ringing downstairs. He heard his mother calling him. Jeff thought about the many different sounds that he could hear.

Then Jeff heard a sound he didn't know. He was a little scared. Jeff listened carefully. He looked under his bed and smiled. It was his kitten playing with a piece of paper!

What Is Sound?

Sound is made by air that **vibrates** (VY-brayts). When something vibrates it moves back and forth quickly. Sound travels in waves through the air to your ears. But people cannot see sound waves in the air. For example, you can hear your alarm clock ringing in the morning, but you can't see the sound that it makes.

Sounds travel through air very quickly. Quiet sounds travel just as quickly as loud sounds, but quiet sounds do not go as far. Sounds travel faster through water, wood, or metal than they do through air.

How Do You Hear?

Hearing is one of your **senses** (SEN-sez). Your senses tell you what is happening to you. Your senses also tell you what is happening around you. You already know that you hear with your ears. Your ears collect sound waves from the air around your head. Each ear on either side of your head helps you tell which direction a sound is coming from. But you hear the sounds that are coming from in front of you the best of all.

Different Ears

Everyone's ears look different on the outside. Your ears certainly look different from the ears of an animal, such as an elephant or a cat! But all ears have important parts that help them to work.

There are three parts to the human ear. Your outer ear is the only part that you can see. The other

two parts are your middle ear and your inner ear. Your middle ear and inner ear are inside your head where you can't see them.

Ears collect sounds and change them into special **signals** (SIG-nulz) that are sent to your **brain** (BRAYN).

Outer Ear

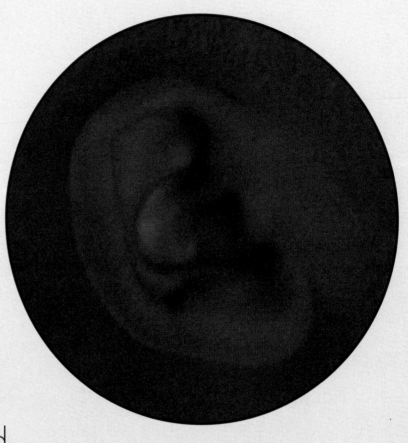

Your outer ear is called the **pinna** (PIN-uh). The bottom of your pinna is the earlobe. Earlobes may be large or very small. The shape and size of your pinna is probably like one of your parents' ears.

Your pinna collects sound waves and carries them to the middle ear. Sound waves travel to your middle ear through a

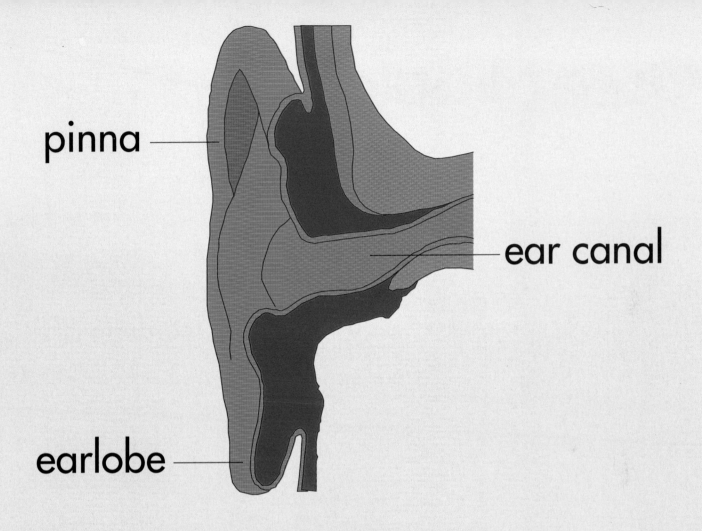

pinna

ear canal

earlobe

tube called the **ear canal** (EER kuh-NAL), which is about ½ inch long.

13

Your Middle Ear

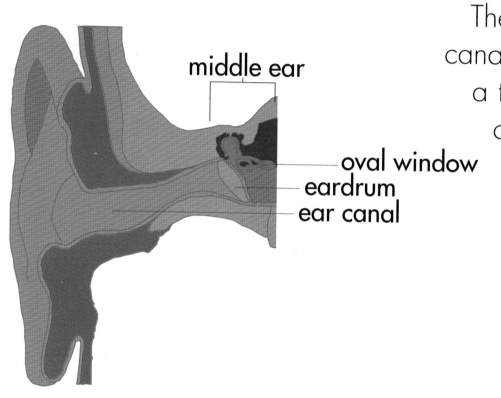

middle ear

oval window
eardrum
ear canal

The end of the ear canal is protected by a thin covering called your **eardrum** (EER-drum). Your eardrum vibrates when sound waves hit it.

The middle ear is on the other side of your eardrum. It is filled

14

with air and three tiny bones. Sound vibrations hitting the eardrum pass through the middle ear along these bones. A small opening called an **oval window** (OH-vul WIN-doh) connects your middle ear and inner ear.

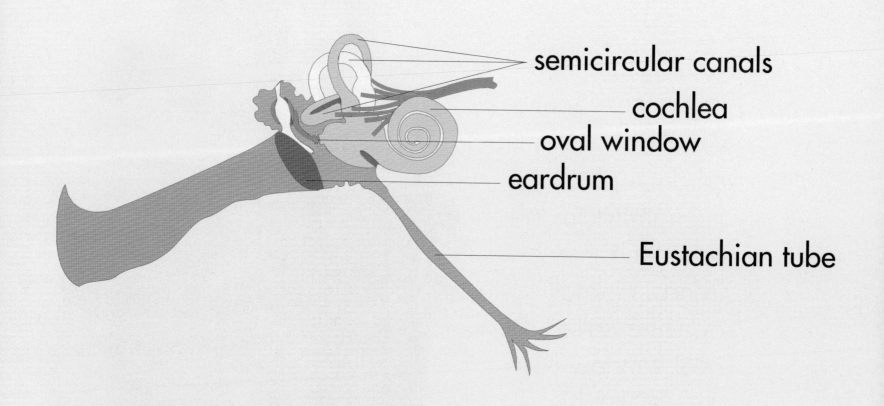

semicircular canals

cochlea

oval window

eardrum

Eustachian tube

16

Your Inner Ear

The main part of your inner ear is a tube called the **cochlea** (KOK-lee-uh). It is shaped like a snail and is about the size of a pea. The cochlea is filled with **fluid** (FLOO-id) and is lined with tiny hairs.

When sound vibrations hit your oval window, they make waves in the cochlea fluid. Loud sounds make big waves and can hurt the hair lining the cochlea. That's why very loud sounds sometimes hurt your ears.

There are three tubes filled with fluid near your cochlea that look like loops. These tubes, called **semicircular canals** (SEM-ee-SIR-kyoo-ler kuh-NALZ), make up the structure called the **labyrinth** (LAB-ih-rinth). Your labyrinth sends messages to your brain to help you keep your balance.

18

Eustachian Tube

Your middle ear does more than help you hear. The **Eustachian tube** (yoo-STAY-shee-un TOOB) connects the middle ear to your throat. Your Eustachian tubes protect your eardrums when air **pressure** (PREH-sher) outside your ears changes. This can happen when you drive up a tall mountain or fly in an airplane. It helps to balance the air pressure on both sides of your eardrums.

Opening your mouth wide, yawning, or chewing gum may balance the air pressure on your eardrums. A buildup of pressure may feel like you have water in your ears. And the change in pressure may feel like a "pop."

Hearing and Your Brain

When sound vibrations reach the fluid in your cochlea, the tiny hairs that line the cochlea change these vibrations into special signals called nerve impulses. These impulses are sent to your brain along the **auditory nerve** (AW-dih-toh-ree NERV). The auditory nerve from each ear leads to your brain. Your brain decides what sounds the vibrations make. Then you can understand what you're hearing.

20

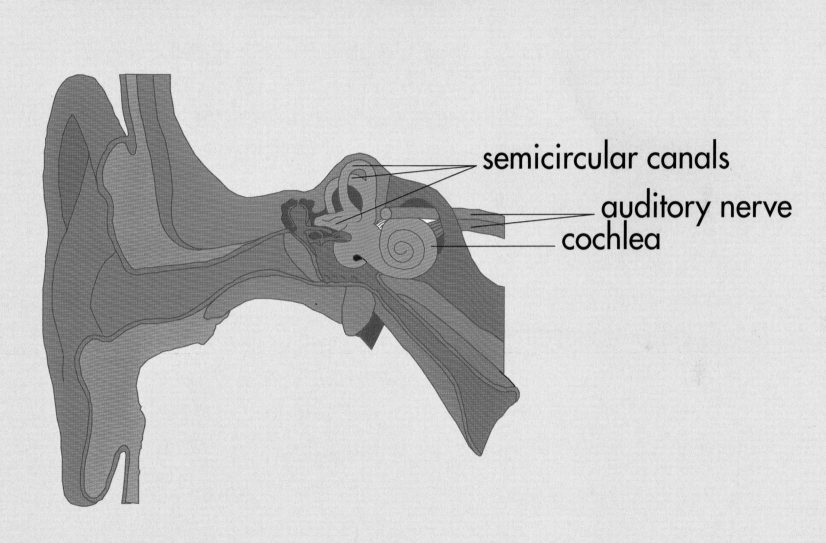

semicircular canals

auditory nerve

cochlea

21

Having Healthy Ears

It's important to take care of your ears. Here are some things to remember about keeping your ears healthy:

3 When you clean your ears, use a cotton swab.

3 Only clean the outside of your ear.

3 Your eardrums are very delicate. They can get hurt easily. Do not try to remove anything from your ears, such as ear wax.

3 Don't put anything into your ears.

3 Don't listen to music too loudly.

By taking care of your ears, you will help to make sure that your hearing lasts for a long time.

Glossary

auditory nerve (AW-dih-tor-ee NERV) The nerve that carries messages about what you hear from your inner ear to your brain.

brain (BRAYN) The main nerve area in your head that controls everything that your body does.

cochlea (KOK-lee-uh) A snail-shaped tube that makes up part of your inner ear.

ear canal (EER kuh-NAL) The tube through which sound travels from the outer ear to the eardrum.

eardrum (EER-drum) A thin layer that stretches across the middle ear.

Eustachian tube (yoo-STAY-shee-un TOOB) A tube that connects each middle ear to the back of your throat.

fluid (FLOO-id) Liquid.

labyrinth (LAB-ih-rinth) A structure made up of three semicircular canals in the inner ear that helps you keep your balance.

oval window (OH-vul WIN-doh) A round opening between the middle ear and the cochlea.

pinna (PIN-uh) The outer part of the ear.

pressure (PREH-sher) A force put on something.

semicircular canal (SEM-ee-SIR-kyoo-ler kuh-NAL) A small tube in the inner ear that helps you keep your balance.

senses (SEN-sez) Ways your body learns what is happening to you and the world around you.

signal (SIG-nul) A sign that gives notice of something.

vibrate (VY-brayt) To move back and forth very quickly.

Index